An Aquarium

An Aquarium

POEMS

Jeffrey Yang

Graywolf Press
SAINT PAUL, MINNESOTA

Publication of this volume is made possible in part by a grant provided by the Minnesota State Arts Board, through an appropriation by the Minnesota State Legislature; a grant from the Wells Fargo Foundation Minnesota; and a grant from the National Endowment for the Arts, which believes that a great nation deserves great art. Significant support has also been provided by the Bush Foundation; Target; the McKnight Foundation; and other generous contributions from foundations, corporations, and individuals. To these organizations and individuals we offer our heartfelt thanks.

Thanks to the editors involved in the following publications for first publishing some of these poems: John Palattella and Peter Gizzi at *The Nation*, Jeffrey Shotts at *Post Road*, and Christopher Mattison and Roland Pease at *Zoland Poetry*.

Published by Graywolf Press
2402 University Avenue, Suite 203
Saint Paul, Minnesota 55114
All rights reserved.

www.graywolfpress.org

Published in the United States of America

ISBN 978-1-55597-513-5

2 4 6 8 9 7 5 3 1
First Graywolf Printing, 2008

Library of Congress Control Number: 2008928257

Cover design: Jeenee Lee Design

Cover art: Ernst Haeckel

for Arjun, on the year of his birth

[*in the light of Michelle Carmelita Alumkal
and of Qingxi, who came after*]

Contents

My pen was creating *myths;* they flowed from my expectant self,
while my mind, hardly seeing what my hand was inventing right before it,
wandered like a sleepwalker among the dark imaginary walls
and submarine theaters of the aquarium. . . .

—PAUL VALÉRY

Abalone

Abalone Rumsen *aulón*
Aristotle auriform Costanoans
cultivated, Brueghel painted,
awabi Osahi dove for
on September 12, 425 A.D.
to please Emperor Ingyō but
was pulled up dead with one clutched in his hand.
Iridescent pearl, nebular swirl, meat all muscle
tastes like rubber. Its gonads a delicacy. Now
universities are funded to study its armor.
All earthly roads lead to war. But remember
haliotis are hemophiliacs—once cut
they bleed to death. Watch your heart.

Anemone

Anemones are warriors, colonizing
rock and reef in ranks. The history
of the world is told thru the eyes
of the colonizer, who takes pleasure in
sticking his finger into an anemone's
mouth until it starves.
For the anemone is the soul
says Saint Theresa
which retreats into itself
in a prayer of recollection.

Aristotle

Aristotle thought eels
"the entrails of the earth."
If "eels" were replaced with
"politicians" this image
would be a guide-
way to a sign. Instead,
it's an instance of
*converting Metaphors
into Proprieties.* And so Browne
doubted Aristotle's leap
into Euripus.
For not understanding tide's
motion, Aristotle recognized
the "imbecility" of reason.

Barnacle

The barnacle settles forever
upside down in its small volcano.
On rock, whale, ship, log—it is
happy anywhere there's current.
The barnacle has the longest penis
of any animal in proportion
to its body size. Happiness
and proportion:
never be ashamed of evolution.

Clownfish

Don't be fooled by a name.
Clownfish are as shy as garibaldi,
and one of the few friends of anemones.
They are practitioners of protandrous
hermaphroditism—for them reproductive;
for man but a dream.

Coelacanth

For centuries aborigines caught
coelacanths. When scientists
caught up to the aborigines, they
made the coelacanth the most famous
fish of our times. This is the nature
of fame: you can live in
a deep undersea cave and
still not escape it. Worse still to pursue it.
Your name or your person, / Which is dearer?
Your name is your person, *nind owiawina.*
Like the coelacanth's spine, fame is hollow.

Crab

Slantwise the crab advances. Poets,
philosophers, the body
politic share different aspects
of this problem.

Dinoflagellate

The glow of crashing waves at night
is caused by dinoflagellates. In great
quantities, they cause ciguatera
and red tides. Without them
the sea would die. Some causes
are invisible to the naked eye.
Strive for equilibrium
rather than neutrality.

Dolphin

The Greeks thought dolphins
were once men. The Chinese
river dolphin was a goddess.
Scientists tell us that if we
rearrange a few of our genes,
we'd become dolphins. Wouldn't
that be real progress!

Eel

Eels are slimy creatures.
But never lie. If they sense
the slightest pretence, they'll
bite off your finger. Carefully
study the hands of politicians.

Flounder

Silent on the sandy seafloor
the flounder sleeps. As you
near its face, perspective
reverses and the flounder
dissimulates a dream of infinity.

Foraminifera

The test of a foraminifera
is its shell—tectinous,
agglutinated, or calcareous
endoskeleton
cytoplasm streams
thru foramen chamber
to chamber of
a single cell, granulo-
reticulose pseudopodia motion,
memory palace of Ōkeanos.
Foraminiferans are found
at all latitudes and marine
environments—foraminiferal white
of the White Cliffs of Dover.
In the pyramids of Giza
Herodotus saw "petrified lentils";
Aldrovandi's eye turned
from Aristotle toward Galileo:
the rhombic shells
have epigenetic stony tubercles.
For Oppen
a test of poetry is
sincerity, clarity, respect. . . .
For Zukofsky *the range of pleasure*
it affords as sight, sound, and intellection.
In a dream
Vishnu visited Appakavi
who received the secrets of
Nannaya's grammar: *Poetry*
is the ultimate learning.

Gamba

See *U.S.*

Garibaldi

Fuori dagli schemi, outside
plans and patterns, Italians
say of Garibaldi. Between pope,
monarchy, or republic he chose
none. Nor did he accept payment.
After one defeat he worked in a candle factory
on Staten Island. Tallow
boredom drove him to sea,
in Lima, he fought rheumatism, fever
then captained the *Carmen* to Canton
with a cargo of guano.
For a unified Italy he gave up everything.
The damsel-
fish is a flaming orange that evokes
the color of dharma.

Google

Google is a sea of consciousness.
As it expands, the sea shrinks.
Like Oz, it is the most knowledgeable
entity that knows nothing. *Information
is originally nothing but difference.*
Surf a wave: knowledge purifies.

Holothurian

Sand biome holothurian home.
To humans, holothurians are
Big Business. Their only defense
is to stiffen and spit out their stomachs.
This is a holy ritual.

Intelligent Design

Self-interest and party politics
define intelligent design
and think tanks. Think
tanks betray
a lack of intelligent design.
Nature describes its own
design. Blessed are the poor.
Can you unravel this paradox?

Jellyfish

Occasionally a crab tires of its slant-
wise ways and stowaways
on the bell of a jellyfish. The bell
pulsates as the jellyfish drifts, drifts
(*in one direction and then in another,*
but generally spreading slantingly)
to the rhythm of antipodal forces.
Food comes and goes; days pass.
Perhaps one day both wash ashore:
the jellyfish dies, and the crab
rediscovers a new world.

Jiang Kui

Jing Wang translates Jiang Kui
of the Northern Song: "In writing poetry,
it is better to strive to be different
from the ancients than to seek to be
identical to them. But better still than
striving to be different is to be bound
to find one's own identity with them,
without striving to identify;
and to be bound to differ with them,
without striving to differ."

Kelp

How easy it is to lose oneself
in a kelp forest. Between
canopy leaves, sunlight filters thru
the water surface; nutrients
bring life where there'd other-
wise be barren sea; a vast eco-
system breathes. Each
being being
being's link.

Lionfish

Lionfish look as pretty as the sun
with rays of fins and spines in striped,
dappled resplendence. What grace
beckons as she swims
in the beauty of appearances.
Get too close tho and you'll burn. At heart
she's a venomous carnivore.

Lobster

Impossible to doubt
the lobster's sorrow. Like a
wordless shudder pain
passes between us. Empty
shell of the subject
inscribes pain's grammar.
Sorrow and pain inflect
one another. Alive
the lobster's been drowned
in fresh water, packed in
sawdust, packed in ice, packed
in polystyrene, packed upright
in gel ice, boiled in brine, slow
frozen, knifed, banded, pegged,
electrocuted, and most recently
hydrostatic pressurized. The U.S.
still absorbs most
of the world's lobsters. War
and protectionism:
two causes of starvation.

Manatee

Manatee Carib *manati*
mammary, Olmec sanctuary,
Guiana girl's grief morphed
watercow (*what terrors un-*
leashed on cows! to manifest mad
cow), gentlest of creatures, Columbo's
sirens, Colombia's most peaceful town.
Manatee, the world's happiest
vegetarian; skin's home to
algae and barnacles; mothers
nurse for twenty-four months; immune
system's inimitable; brain contains more
gray matter than humans', *homo*
sapiens their only natural predators
yet they welcome us with open limbs.
O Great Ancestors! Teach us
how to love our enemies.

Mola Mola

After Adam's nomenclature
Linnaeus disposuit, *Tetraodon mola*
Mola Mola millstone mill-
stone grinds
mollusca, arthropoda
crustacea, beak-plate Mola
not four-toothed but four-gilled, thick-
skinned scaleless parasitic mambo
of Eocene traces, heterogeneous spaces
Giant Sun-
ship clavus rudder, twin-fins
stone sails temperate waters
from Agulhas Current to Yellow Sea
Algeria to Vietnam
cow-eyed Mola retroflects
self
splits nomen:
Visayan putol cut short, Hawaiian Makua parent
progenitor, Schwimmender Kopf swimming
head, Pez cabeza, Headfish, Moon-
fish, 曼波 Manbô long wave, Almindelig
klumpfish, Ay baligi, Cá Mặt trăng,
Tunglfiskur, Girasole, Korshid-mahi-e-oghyanoosi,
Lua, Bucan, Bezador, Pixxitambur, Pixxiluna,
Bot, Boloublè, Orelhão, Ra-a-ta-a-
hu-i-hu-i, Morski mesec, Φεγγαρόψαρο Fegaropsaro,
Opesee-sonvis, Qamar, Sol,
Maanvis, Månefisk, Poisson lune,
Pescio meua, Pesciu meua, Pesce bala,
Möhkäkala, Mullacchia, Niffâkha, луна-рыба luna-ryba,
Pervane baligi, Peixe-roda, Rolim,

Samoglów, Mánafiskur, Môle,
and Chinese 翻 車 魚 fan che yu, fish flipped car
or, scoop-wheel, *the motive force*
Needham wrote
of Su Song's armillary sphere.

Mormyrid

Mormyrids live in the rivers of Africa
and on tomb walls of the ancient Egyptians.
It is said Set's image could be
that of a mormyrid. Or is the mormyrid's
image that of Set? the way
man is the image of God?
Scientists exploit
the mormyrid's unique electrical
properties to test water.

Nautilus

Chamber after chamber
of the nautilus
shell grows in a perfect
logarithmic spiral.
In unseen depths
a life obedient aspires
like silent
cephalopodic music.

Nudibranch

You must be patient
to find a nudibranch
in a tidepool. Pretend
the tidepool is history
and the nudibranch a
lacuna of history. When
you do find a nudibranch,
its brilliant cerata mane
blinds you with truth—
not the possession of truth
but the effort in struggling to attain it
brings joy to the searcher—
you're never the same again.

Oarfish

Oar Old Norse *Ar*
fisc Midgard Jörmungandr
ourobouros oarfish Elihu
Vedder's sleeping serpent
a sleep of the heavens suggestive of thunder.
God's mystery *at once center*
and circumference
Sor Juana induces *Todas las cosas*
salen de Dios. . . . But the oarfish?
One rare sighting
in the Sargasso Sea (weed
tar clumps, Euripized
plastic): "flat as a knife blade
snakelike head capped
by a rooster's coxcomb."
Echoes Lawrence at the Anapo:
look, look at him!
With his head up, steering like a bird!
He's a rare one, but he belongs. . . .
Oor Oort Cloud sphere
oarismos amor gentle sweetness
pillow whisperings: *omnia*
uincit Amor: et nos cedamus Amori
other shore oared, angled
spar, silver
skin coruscates
rhombic crystals of guanine.

Octopus

Tikopians believe the octopus
is both a mountain with tentacle-
streams, and the sun
with its rays, so should not be eaten.
The mystery of metaphor is
nearly lost to us, as if
only the illusion of metaphor
remains. Or the myth of metaphor.
Or metaphor without ikon.
Rousseau writes:
The first speech was all in poetry.
Or poetry's reasoning
was the first figure
of speech. Palin
genesis of word (*butter
bird*) mind's
forms, reveals
mind ether, spirit
unhindered.

Orca

The Chinese call orcas "tiger
whales"; Pliny likened them to
warships; a *Yuukara* song of the Saru
Ainu goes, "Killer whale, god of the ocean,
please bring more than one and a half
whales every year. Then, I'll
be pleased to give my sweet daughter as a bride."
High on the Nazca Desert is the orca's image.
The Tlingit are also matrilineal. Taxonomically
the orca's a whale within a dolphin within a whale.
And never known to harm a human
unless forced to do chlorinated circus
tricks, in which case they die young.

Parrotfish

The life phases of a parrotfish
are expressed in colors. By day,
the parrotfish replenishes coral reef
sands, and by night spins
its mucous cocoon bed-
room. Is this art's archetype
abstracted from politics?
Picasso thought abstraction a cul-de-
sac. The CIA loved Abstract
Expressionism. Hockney: "I
don't think that there is really such a thing
as abstraction." Langer: "All genuine art
is abstract."
What
do you think parrot-
fish?

Peysonnel

Coral pearl ambergris
wealth of the sea in antiquity
the first overfished by the third
century, mind's
vegetable or stone
until Peysonnel's enquiries
circa 1719
off the coasts of Provence
Barbary he discovers
the fabric of animals . . . une
petite ortie ou poulpe. 1727:
the Paris Royal Academy of Sciences
condemns Peysonnel's findings
so he boards ship as naval surgeon
exiles himself to Guadeloupe where
he continues his investigations
and in 1751, 7 years before his death,
he submits a 400-quarto-page treatise
to the Royal Society of London
(10 chapters on coral, 8 *dissertations on*
vermicular tubes including the sponge)
that is "extracted and translated"
by Mr. William Watson who conch-
ologically cries, *O altitudo divitiarum!,*
and concludes his account:
". . . the Royal Society is greatly obliged
to M. de Peysonnel, for
his transmitting this manuscript,
which I consider as a very valuable literary
present." Thus Peysonnel's fragment
in the natural history of memory, wherein

today's observations become tomorrow's
definitions, endless reef
embayed by language, Ponge's
l'amphibiguité de la Nature
Qian glosses with *yi* 易.

Quahog

Quahog Narragansett *poquaûhock*
closed shell people
of the narrow point used as wampum,
wine-dark suckauhock ornaments.
Pelag confused with Queequeg.
Read its rings like the rings
of a tree. At the Assowamset Swamp,
Metacomet fell—wife, son sold
as slaves. While the missionary
would say: *Wáme pitch*
chíckauta mittaùke. Before long
the whole world shall be burnt.

Quincunciall

If all the trees were pens, the oceans ink . . .

—SURAH LUQMAN [31:27]

Arabic, Persian, Sogdian, Greek tongues
of the world-state at Madīnat al-
Salām, al-Fārābī, between caliphates, clothed
in the brown garb of the Sufis relates
the soul's 5 faculties, the 5
ajzā of *al-madīna al-fādila,* root
of obedience, contiguous others
one professes
a *felicity of association* that is
the virtuous city society   state   polis.
Out of the Garden of Cyrus
Browne adumbrates, *in Quincucem directa,* Jaar
Eden flow groves of rhombic viridescence
systatic harmony of soul, x reflected circle
fenestrae reticulatae, window-
light framed like nets, khamsa lozenge
seapoose whirl, the oud's perfection in 5
strings, the 64 hexagrams circulate the 5 elements
at diametral verti-cities, *al-ahl* of a nation
so exact that it yeelds not to other Countreys.

Remora

R is for Remora, for:
"The mightiest power
does not always prevail. A ship
may be detained by a small remora,"
quotes Borges of
Diego de Saavedra Fajardo's
Political Emblems (1640).

Rexroth

R is for Rexroth
the contemplator at the center
of many universes, in a grain
of sand. How can this aquarium
compare to his bestiary? As snow
begins to fall again
over the land, the ocean
shrinks, expands, hardly
liminal how things are, how
things have come to be
our history, *the long pain
of history*. No need
to dismiss his faults
against his words
earned
by his life lived
as a radical intellectual, a populist
ecologist, a pacifist between
the dragon
and the unicorn
in eternal conversation.

Riftia

Millennia after millennia Riftia
lived in peace. Then
1977, a year after Mao's death
during the Ogaden War,
scientists descended the ocean's
depths and discovered
more positive ignorance:
a world
no hominid had seen before
at 350°C, sea-
floor rifts black
smoke pours
Riftia blooms red
plumes. Existence.
Lightlessness.
Collection,
dissection, experiment
sequence. Quetzalcoatl
bleeds.

Seahorse

It is said an encounter with a seahorse
in a dream is an encounter with the un-
conscious. Is this because both
evoke delicate armor? Beneath
history is another history we've made
without *knowing* it. No bit's
small enough to harness. Ritual
dance, her ovipositor in his belly
pouch [. . .] progeny disperse.

Shark

The fossil record of sharks reaches
far past the dinosaurs. To the Hawaiians
mano, god and messenger of the gods;
to the Mayans *xoc* fish carved glyphs.
At Yaxchilàn, Lady Xoc bleeds her tongue
with a rope of thorns, opening
the way to the ancestors. And xoc of Pacal
Palenque could signify a foreigner?
From the Gulf of Mexico up
the Mississippi beyond where the people
of Poverty Point preceded, xoc swim.
Every doorway tells a story.

Sponge

We have yet to understand
the mystery of the sponge. A phylum
unto itself, sponge
fossils found
in Doushantuo phosphorite
are the most ancient of
multicellular animals. The sponge lives
at all depths of the sea, an array of colors,
shapes, textures, canals, Goethe's
paradise, lacks coincidence. In reality,
a sponge isn't a parasite unless
it's human. Then it doesn't purify but
withers the world. Remember
Kropotkin's mutual trust and support,
Proudhon's exchange, Gandhi's boycotts.

Squid

In the U.S., Nemo's *Nautilus*
was attacked by a giant cuttle-
fish squid—*What a freak of nature!*
a bird's beak on a mollusc!—
But a friend tells me that
in Mexico it was a giant octopus.
How profound translation
shapes our dreams! And dream
a silent translation of a dream
the way squids chromatophorically
communicate. And translation
a dream of One. *Translate,*
follow up on, follow after . . .

Starfish

One feels a *sainte-terrer* walking
the starfish shore. The soul
delighteth in decussate symmetry
dwells quincuncially. Without a word
prayer elevates the heart. Star-
fish have neither brain nor heart.
Perhaps they are pure intellect of
soul pure coincidence pure
feeling clinging to the rocks of Paradise.
Far from living water the soul desiccates.

Tarpon

Tarpon Miskito *tahpam*
as mystifying today as in pre-
history. Stationary, migratory;
saltwater, freshwater; solitary,
social; big eyes big scales, capable
of gulping air, silver sides sun glint
daisy-chain foreplay! Read its otolith like
a quahog's rings, time's
hidden constancy. Lep-
tocephali larvae
translucent ribbons with fangs drift
to estuary, reach almost three
centimeters then within one day
shrink suddenly to the physiognomy
of an adult . . . and fly away. Bosch
fish metamorphosis, Mother
Nature unending
miracle, divinity
tamed.

[Time (Outside the Quincunx)]

Philosophy's shadow: poetry. Poetry's
shadow: philosophy. Poetry art: revolt.
Perspective absorbs perspective: time.
Tide: *the love of the moon for the earth.*

Triggerfish

The humuhumunukunukuapua'a
is Hawaii's native triggerfish. Pua'a
means pig, one of many sacred animals
born from the *Kumulipo* night—*O*
ke akua ke komo, 'a'oe komo kanaka.
The god enters, man cannot enter
until the age passed
from *po* to *ao,* cosmogony to
cosmology, Kalakaua to Bastian to
Frobenius Pohaku, flower-
bird gatherer, gatherer
of seeds, muan bpo spirits who
propitiate Heaven, who believe
one thinks with one's heart,
harmony kaona, Pound
testing the overtones
from his distant pithos, *esse*
as citizen of cosmos [implosion],
of Pohaku's dream: poetry, echo of
Aquinas happiness: *the perfect*
activity of the intellect depends
on right understanding, divine
quiddity, around us, Flora
Fauna fades, bay
slick with sun-
screen, humuhumunukunukuapua'a's
home-reef we cannot recreate.

U.S.

The U.S. is a small fish
with a false head; or a big fish
with false scales; or a dream
of the perfect fish
that turns into nightmare;
or a fish with a mouth as big
as an atom; or a secret fish
named Morgan, Mellon, Carlyle,
Rockefeller; or a fish that eats
its own tail; or an illegal
fish with respect to its own laws;
or a fish with a circulatory system
of black gold; or an army of robot fish;
or a fish that acts like it's the only existing fish;
or a Japanese fish; or an Israeli fish;
or a fish that pollutes the whole sea;
or a fish that consumes the whole sea;
or a fish that ate its ancestors; or a
fish with a double life; or a fish
out of water hooked up to a respirator;
or a fried fish; or a fat fish; or a red fish;
or a fish unhappy with its own skin;
or a tin-straw-lion fish; or a Shiite Muslim
fish with a Protestant upbringing;
or a blind fish swimming thru a minefield;
or an extinct fish in a museum;
or a fish with fry full of hope;
or not really a fish but a gamba.

Vacuum

Aquinas head down in a vacuum
          Aristotle which way in a vacuum?
Sacrum, sacrum, inluminatio coitu.

—E.P., CANTO XXXVI

Vishnu

Where is your sword
Discrimination?
Draw it and slash
Delusion to pieces.
—KRISHNA

Vishnu preserver, sustainer, absolute
Vishnu whose three strides turned
    emptiness to cosmos
Vishnu Matse Avatar leviathan
Vishnu Field-Knower, incarnate in
    Krishna, charioteer who reveals
        the blessed hymn of karma yoga
Vishnu whose tenth descent
    will restore dharma again
Vishnu Self's soul, ten thousand
    manifestations
Vishnu divine lotus dreamer
Vishnu Ishvara vision *mattah sarvam pravartate*
Vishnu Cloud blue
Vishnu life-force sea
    of milk sacred shankha shell pours out *samudra*
        manthan sound of creation
Vishnu's sleep we live

White Whale

Round and round we wheel
around the White Whale
in a braided cord
of good and evil,
        till self's
freed
from ego.

Xi-Turtle

Follow the third guideway thru
the Eastern Mountains, pass
the Desert of Shifting Sands to
Tiptoe Peak, bare of plants
and trees but full of jade and giant
snakes, you'll find Deep Lake
where the sacred Xi-Turtle dwells.
The markings on its shell foretell;
its stomach emanates strange sounds.
Says Master Zhuang: *What people
know is inferior to what they do not know.*

Xiangjun

Follow the twelfth guideway thru
the Middle Mountains to the realm
of the Nine Rivers where Xiao
flows into Xiang and tear-stained
bamboo grows. In this place four
thousand years ago the Xiangjun
drowned themselves—two daughters
of Yao, wives of Shun. Not even
geese can bear their water-spirit
sorrow. Tang poet Qian Qi:
Why rashly turn back   once at the Xiao-Xiang
Blue-green waters bright sand moss on both banks
Twenty-five strings plucked on moonlit nights   an
unbearable   pure melancholy   so they take flight

X-ray fish

You can see straight thru
an X-ray fish to its heart.
We are just as transparent
so be true, gentle, honest, just . . .

Yingshao

Follow the third guideway thru
the Western Mountains to reach
Scholartree River Peak covered
with green realgar, cinnabar, Lang-
gan Stone, yellow gold, silver, and jade.
There you'll find the Supreme Deity's
Garden of Peace, tended by Yingshao
who has the body of a horse, a human
face, tiger's stripes, and bird's wings.
His home is the Four Seas he
circles thru, while making sounds
"like reading books aloud."
Of the unknown
heed Daoist Ge Hong:
Never enter a mountain lightly.

Zhi-Fish

Follow the first guideway thru
the Northern Mountains west
of Zhuhuai waters to Ruckus River
in which Zhi-Fish thrive. Dog head
fish body babytalk . . . If you think
you're insane, eat one quick
for Zhi-Fish restore your psyche.

Zi-Fish

Follow the second guideway thru
the Southern Mountains two
thousand four hundred and ten li
past Willow Peak east to Floating
Jade Mountain, source
of Broomstraw River that empties
into Juqu Lake. There you'll find
plenty of Zi-Fish, a fish as ordinary
as a mullet. "But it depends on me
to make a mullet strange," Guo Pu
would say. If you think
you've wasted a trip,
think again.

Zooxanthellae

The Chinese world archetype
can be compared to a chariot: Heaven
the canopy, earth the cart, magick
square of 45 circles, 1 to 9 linked
center of 5, each side and diagonals of
3 links sums 15 concealing
a science of the mind. River
of causes to investigate
ideal order that underlies, an
anthropology, a poetry the witness
testifies and doesn't testify, a poetry
of the jury. 7 years
after '45, the first hydrogen bomb
was detonated at Enewetak. Preparations
had begun less than a year after
'45 with Operation Crossroads
at Bikini Atoll. The native people
were forcibly moved from their ancestor home
by the U.S. government, atoll to atoll, while they
starved: Bikini to Rongerik to Kwajalein to Kili.
Able and Baker, 2 Hiroshima size tests,
contaminated the water and a fleet
of WWII ships in Bikini's lagoon. Then came
Operation Sandstone at Enewetak, 3 atomic
tests. Then Operation Greenhouse, 4 atomic
tests. Then Operation Ivy,
the first H-bomb test, and all the while
more forced migrations: Enewetak to Kwajalein to
Ujelang; Rongelap to Lae; Wotho to Lae;
Ujelang to . . . The government

named the H-Bomb Mike, the blast
vaporized Elugelab Island: "Probably more
than 100 million tons of material were dislodged
and thrown into the air, great waves were
sent out that rolled over nearby islands, and a
huge mushroom cloud rose to a height of
130,000 feet in just 15 minutes. Mike was indeed
a superdevice, estimated to have a yield of about 5
megatons or the equivalent of 250 Hiroshima-type
atomic bombs." Then 9 years after '45 came Operation
Castle, created by Joint Task Force 7: the Army, Navy, Air
Force, contractors ("primarily from the firm Holmes
and Narver"), and Department of Defense people were
all involved, along with 28 U.S. servicemen that formed
a Radiation Safety team. This time people of surrounding
islands weren't moved and Bravo was detonated on the ground
of Bikini Atoll, March 1st 06:45 a.m. Kilo time, rather than
above ground "for minimal fallout" tho all previous
tests, like those in Nevada, were detonated above ground, and tho
weather conditions were downgraded to "unfavorable." Also
nearby at the time of the blast was a 23-man
Japanese fishing boat, the *Lucky Dragon,* that risked
being caught by the U.S. Navy in Trust Territory waters.
Uranium 238, lithium deuteride, uranium 235, metal mechanisms and
circuitry "erupted into a blinding white force of monstrous proportions
of heat and radioactivity. Accompanied by a deafening, thunderous
roar and an earth and sea-moving high-pressure blast, by 06:55 a.m.,
Bravo's giant nuclear cloud reached a peak of 21.6 miles tall. The yield
of Bravo is estimated to be near 20 megatons, or the equivalent of 1,000
Hiroshima-type bombs." Wind spread the cloud, particles fell, JTF 7

crewmembers aboard ships 30 miles east of Bikini were ordered to go below deck, the ships fled south, fallout snow fell on the *Lucky Dragon* fishermen who caught it on their tongues, and then on the people of Rongelap and Ailinginae, and then on the Radiation Safety team at Rongerik tho some were in planes monitoring the explosion, and then over Utirik and Ailuk. . . . Children played in the snow. 34 hours later the 28 Americans were safe on ship after visiting Rongelap by amphibious plane and measuring the dangerously high levels of radiation. They left the people with 4 words: "Don't drink the water." 1 day after the Americans evacuated, JTF7 converged on Rongelap and Ailinginae to tell the people that they must leave immediately, or would die. Then the people of Utirik were evacuated, but not the people of Ailuk, tho Ailuk is nearly the same distance to Bikini as Utirik. The U.S. Atomic Commission issued a statement to the press calling Bravo "a routine atomic test" and that "There were no burns. All reported well." In the following years, doctors from the Brookhaven National Laboratory, run by the U.S. Department of Energy, carefully documented the "most valuable ecological radiation study on human beings. Since only small amounts of radioisotopes are necessary for tracer studies, the various radionuclides present on the island can be traced through the food and into the human being, where the tissue and organ distributions, biological half-times, and excretion rates can be studied." Tests and experiments were performed on the people; "some patients today still do not understand that their entire thyroids were removed" (tho human radiation experiments began long before as described in Welsome's *Plutonium Files*). Project 4.1 was planned in New Mexico months before Bravo, and was called "Study of Response of Human Beings Exposed to Significant Beta and Gamma Radiation due to Fallout from High Yield Weapons." 2 years after Bravo came Operation Redwing. Then Operation Hardtack. Then. . . . At least 67 atomic tests were performed. During these tests, the scientists discovered significant quantities of algae living in 2 places: in the sand and on dead coral; and inside the polyp tissues and skeletons of the coral themselves. This algae is a kind of dinoflagellate that lives symbiotically with the coral, supplying it with oxygen and nutrients thru photosynthesis while transforming calcium ions from the ocean into calcium carbonate the coral uses to grow. In return the coral provides the algae with a safe home and access to food like carbon dioxide and nitrogen. Here finally was proof that tropical reef communities operated according to the same fundamental laws of nature that govern other food chains, built on a foundation of plants, and subsisting in an evolutionary relationship intimately defined by mutualism. The algae is called zooxanthellae.

Thus there is something in us that can be without us and
will be after us though indeed it hath no history what it was
before us and cannot tell how it entered into us.

—SIR THOMAS BROWNE

JEFFREY YANG works as an editor at New Directions Publishing. His recent books include translations of Su Shi's *East Slope* and a Tang-Song dynasty collection of poems called *Rhythm 226*. He lives in Beacon, New York.

This book was designed by Rachel Holscher. It is set in Arno Pro type by BookMobile Design and Publishing Services, and manufactured by Versa Press on acid-free paper.